Stone in My Pocket

Poems and Images of Maine

Moody Mountain Writers

Mary Jane Martin
Debbie Mitchell
Selkie O'Mira
Janet L. G. G. Smith

Best Wishes,
Janet L. G. G. Smith

Moody Mountain Press
17 Benner Drive
Belfast, ME 04915
www.moodymountainwriters.com

The rights to each individual poem and photograph are retained by each individual artist. No part of this book may be used or reproduced in any manner whatsoever without written permission from the publisher and artists, except in the case of brief quotations embodied in critical essays, articles or reviews.

Grateful appreciation for her support, as well as this acknowledgement, are due to the editor of *Animus*, Annie Farnsworth, where two of these poems first appeared: "March Mind Gardens", *Volume 1*, and "Saturday Canvas", *Volume 5*. Additional grateful acknowledgement goes to the editors of *A Sense of Place: Collected Maine Poems*, where "The True Story of Santa's Demise" first appeared. Thank You. Janet L. G. G. Smith

"Bob" first appeared in *Prism*, Spring 1997, published by Emerson College Press.

© 2007 Moody Mountain Writers
ISBN 978-0-9795235-0-2

Back cover photograph of
Moody Mountain Writers
by Ken Mitchell
All other photographs
by Debbie Mitchell

Cover Photo *Fisherman*
by Debbie Mitchell
Cover Design
by Moody Mountain Writers
Ray Estabrook Printing Services
Printed in Maine

Moody Mountain Writers

We met by chance at a local poetry reading in Camden, Maine. Sharing a desire to support each other's work, we formed Moody Mountain Writers, named for one of the lovely hills that overlook our gathering place. Once a week we get together to read aloud, share and critique our writing. Our enthusiasm for each other's poetry has led to this book.

A long-time resident, life-long Mainer and two newcomers to the Pine Tree State, we feature this common habitat in many of our poems. *Stone in My Pocket* is a tribute to this place we call home.

Many of us who visit Maine leave with a longing to return. We may carry home a small token to extend our experience. Some of us do return - or never leave - finding in these granite hills, forests and rocky shores a pace we can live with, a beauty that offers consolation, a liveliness that awakens.

Whether you are a fifth-generation Mainer or 'from away', we hope that you will enjoy these images of Maine and carry one with you, like a stone in your pocket. We offer them to you with joy and gratitude.

Table of Contents

Clean	vi
Saturday Canvas	1
Coming Home	2
Hope	4
The Opposite of a Fence	5
Haiku	6
Haiku	7
March Mind Gardens	7
Sea Farm	8
Some Days	9
Time	10
Harbor	11
Haiku	12
Gwenivere	13
Insight	14
A Granddaughter's Vigil	15
Pops	16
Immortality	17
Afternoon Nap	18
Growing Up	19
Haiku	20
Saturday Nights after World War II	21
Exposure	22
One Swallow, A Summer Does Not Make	23
Hands Like These	24
Stone in My Pocket	25
The Bubbles	26
Enough	27
My Friend	28
An Old Picture	29
Oh, you brilliant children!	30
Simple Memories	31
Haiku	32
August Recollection – Age Eight	33

Memories of Camp	34
Inside Out	36
Global Warming	37
Good	38
Haiku	40
Ash Trees in Autumn	41
Seasoning	42
Mirrored Fangs	44
Camp	45
Otto	46
Early Fall	48
Concords	49
Sweater-Buttoned Day	50
Leaves on Grass	51
The Last Day of October	52
November First	53
Hot Apple Pie	54
Bob	56
Accidents	58
Bare Room	59
Route 235	60
Blank Page	61
The True Story of Santa's Demise	62
Quiet	64
Nor'easter	65
They Say You Can't Go Home Again	66
Waiting	68
January Lifts Her Smile	69
Why Winds Rage	70
Wood, Fire, and Stone	71
It's about time	72
Midwinter Treat	73
Memories	74

Clean

Janet L. G. G. Smith

Saturday Canvas

Magical mayflies swarm
their Pied Piper tease,
lead the red-capped man
and his eager grandson,
who grips a new rod and reel
in his white-knuckled hand.

With silent steps on spongy moss
they make their way toward
the Great River of Big Fish Stories,
where sun-sparkled water
pounds against boulders,
becomes rainbow foam.

Arriving, they seek the perfect pool
to flick forth the Gray Ghost,
to raise their silver lines against air
in a whisper as ancient as the stars.
Tireless arms practice the motions
in a pool of shimmering scales.

Soon, success in a soft net.

Laying his rod aside, the boy
draws in a long, proud breath,
released only by his grandfather's smile.
With care, they release the salmon,
then dry their red-socked feet
by a crackling orange fire;

their story becomes an amulet,
forged into memory
by the telling and re-telling.

Selkie O'Mira

Coming Home

Stopping by L.L. Bean's on my way back
from the airport, having coffee at their
Dew Drop Inn –

with a sense of belonging, even though They wouldn't
think so. I order coffee and a croissant, which might be
made with lard –

I don't care.

Barbara, that's Bah-bra, asks Do I want it heated,
Do I need a knife and fork, Am I going to
walk around or sit and rest –

I'll sit.

I can still hear her talking, asking the same
friendly questions with her strong Maine accent,
as though she wants everyone to feel at home –

I feel comforted.

I could decide to be a Mainer, even though
They don't accept self-declared citizenship.
I could immerse myself many more years in this
beautiful place, regardless of proprietary rights.

For I love these mountains, I love these ponds,
I love the sacred sea, scattered with islands
and polka-dot buoys –

I love these people.

Selkie O'Mira

Twenty-some years I have lived in this place,
longer than any other – in a few years
it will be more than half my life.

That's okay with me –
that's definitely okay . . .

That's downright wicked good okay by me.

Mary Jane Martin

Hope

This spring

I hope lilacs bloom longer
I hope my dog avoids muddy puddles
I hope our troops come home

This spring I hope

    But...

lilacs never bloom long enough
dogs always leave muddy prints and
our troops' Commander-in-Chief is one stubborn fool

Well, you know what they say

    Hope springs...

The Opposite of a Fence

I come from small plots of land
Houses crammed into canyons
with roofs of shingle

I come from the land of many people
Eyes averted
they seldom acknowledge

I come from freeways
Herds of cars squeal
Follow white lines and shoot off exits

What I want is the woods
Long meadows of hay
turning golden after the green of July

What I need is a farm pond still
with geese swimming
A gathering of grinning trees

What I'm learning is silence
and speckled sky of night
Wind in dancing tree tops

What I give you is a tree frog
A raven circling
and the sound of my heart
beating to a rhythm
I've almost found

Mary Jane Martin

Amber eyes keenly
follow the erratic path
of the fickle bee.

Winter laughs at spring
creaking beneath purple snow
while birch trees shiver

March Mind Gardens

Through winter freeze
and house bound tears,
catalogues and mind gardens
sustain.

During wild winds
and gray day emptiness,
pots on the windowsills
hold me hopeful.

Later, seedlings struggle when
moved from bright windows
to their earth wombs,
fight to take hold.

Gentle spring rains
moisten the soft soil
produce strong plants,
far from their birthplace –
in March Mind Gardens.

Sea Farm

Debbie Mitchell

Some Days

This is one of those days
The words don't come
They sit, full of molasses
in the back of your throat
And the dog wants a walk
and the laundry needs to be done
and you read some other poet's
beautiful words
and you want to stop trying

Some days you have to be
gentle to yourself
Hold your face with your two hands
Look in the mirror and say
Enough, enough of this today
Let yourself off the hook
Take a long bath with a
short book

Eat a pint of ice cream for lunch
Buy cookies in a red paper bag
for an afternoon snack
Pour tea from a flowered pot
and lie with your legs
stretched over the arm
of your favorite chair

Let the late afternoon sun
set without whining
Open your arms to the darkness
Give a lap to the dog
who can tell you
that nothing else matters
except this moment
with him licking your face

Mary Jane Martin

Time

My watch has stopped
But I need time
      to finish my book
      to go to Paris
to say I'm sorry

Harbor

Mary Jane Martin

In a still moment
when a paw gently intrudes,
my thoughts unravel.

Gwenivere

Long after she had gone
after all the tears
to be shed
were shed
and long after we
stopped listening
for her,
we found her footprints
high
on a dusty shelf
as if she had marked
a trail we could follow.

Insight

Janet L. G. G. Smith

A Granddaughter's Vigil

Walking down a lane of shade trees
to my mailbox, I see a green-haired teen
sitting on top of a picnic table
under a budding apple tree.

I know her, this soulful girl
of multiple body-piercings,
recognize her slouch as body music
to a bereft and painful song.

I gently step onto the new green lawn,
born under snow this early spring,
hope to help Sophie in some small way –
as the counselor I was, or the neighbor I am.

This frail waif keeps vigil in the front yard
of her green-thumbed grandmother,
the one she loved like no other,
who yesterday fell to the floor and died.

Sophie tells me, while choking on her sobs,
that she cried all day yesterday,
then fell into the eye of her storm
and in that white calm remembered

this line from a poem:
Children's voices, wild with pain,
Surely, she will come again! *

*The Merman, by Matthew Arnold

Debbie Mitchell

Pops

Last night Emily
took Ken's two index fingers
wrapped a pudgy hand
around each one

and walked
one curled foot
after the other
into the living room

With body bent over
he talked to her
about his childhood
About walking to school
ten miles
barefoot
through the snow

I watched
as she took each step
pausing to look up at him
as they rounded the corner

The two of them suspended
between birth and death
as if they had known each other
forever

Immortality

I pop corn, start a movie, settle in.
Then guilt finds a crevice, niggles:
> *Ah, Mom's fried dough!*
> *She would grab a hank of bread dough,*
> *fry it in lard, then slather it*
> *with butter and molasses.*
> *Today, tiny fat gobs*
> *course through my arteries,*
> *sometimes create road blocks.*

So, I turn off the movie,
drag my old body
from couch-potato position
to pseudo-athletic stance.
Then I hit the hills,
pump my calf muscles
until they bellow
like a hostile herd of cows.
A mile up the road
my second wind alights
and endorphins boogie
throughout my brain.
I'm on cruise-control.
Suddenly, the distant *Vroooooom*
of a loud muffler startles. In a split-second,
a flash of long red hair blazes in the sun
and a low-slung convertible soars past me
at about sixty-in-a-forty. I suck in some air.
Brake lights blaze red on the unforeseen sharp curve
as hysterical, screeching tires barely hold their grip.
Without so much as a pause, she speeds away –
her belief in her immortality intact.

Afternoon Nap

Growing Up

In my first 10 years
>I cried as much as I needed
>Ate most of what was offered
>Sang old songs with my father

In my teens
>I learned very little
>Looked for love all over
>Held myself less than I should have

In my twenties
>I married for love and adventure
>Bore babies because I wanted them
>Cooked chicken in too many ways

In my thirties
>I struggled to take in air
>Thought I was losing my mind
>Ran to keep from dying

In my forties
>I smiled a lot more often
>Found I could earn money
>Held hands as much as I wanted

In my fifties
>I touched my first grandchild
>Learned to love my mother
>Donated my breasts to cancer

In my sixties
>I will read by the wood fire
>Eat more wildflowers
>inhale spring

Mary Jane Martin

In early spring
when leaves turn the color of limes,
my smile puckers.

Janet L. G. G. Smith

Saturday Nights after World War II

Sinatra crooned from the radio
in Gram's smoke-filled kitchen
where Gramp and my father,
two uncles and four laughing aunts,
stood around, sucked on their Camels,
drank their whiskey *straight-up*.

Dad whipped off the tablecloth
embroidered with strawberries,
picked up the cards, then snapped,
shuffled and dealt Betty Grable,
her bosom high, legs sleek and long,
glad to watch her slide across the table.

In the front room of overstuffed chairs,
I fought my cousins, big or small,
for the green chair by the doorway,
then pretended to read *Nancy Drew*,
instead, listened to
the grownups' wobbly-words.

I sifted every tone, nuance and silence
through the sieve of my mind
while waiting in great anticipation
for my soldiers to swallow
enough whiskey to drown the enemy
and win the war.

Then, when the great sounds
of Tommy Dorsey's, *Boogie-Woogie*,
shook the old Philco, my family
would leap from their chairs,
dance around and around
in their frenzy of liberation.

Debbie Mitchell

Exposure

It is early morning
and light filters through
trees at a deep angle
making the shadows long

A moose walks by the cabin at 5:45
and my husband reaches
for his camera
When I think of this place

where I want to grow old
I see my husband's smile
and the face of the moose
as they watch each other

Then the camera shutter clicks –
the moose turns and moves away
And I see the man I love
standing on pine needles

still frozen
in the mist of early morning
eye to the camera
unable to breathe

Janet L. G. G. Smith

One Swallow, A Summer Does Not Make
(An Old Proverb)

My mind is soaked in depression
after six days of relentless rain,
when respite,
dressed as a slab of spring sun,
stirs my sullen senses.

For the first time in six days
I see purple martins on their bungalow
and a crow leap from my compost pile,
banana peel in talons. He flies high
with his fool's gold, unaware of his folly.

And I see just one fork-tailed swallow on a post.

Later, on a line between two tall pines,
twelve pair of blue overalls kick in the breeze
like a chorus line of farmers,
and the Herefords beyond the stonewall
slog their way through a meadow of buttercups.

I taste this fresh, yellow-spring day,
swallow it whole,
feel the generous grace of it
course through my entire body.
Grabbing a book, I head for the deck,

but, wait! Black clouds now sweep the sky
again, and the breeze succumbs, lies flat.
Stillness stirs up the black flies
who soon lust for my blood.

Debbie Mitchell

Hands Like These

I dig in the garden all afternoon
then struggle to stand
These wrinkled hands I use
they belong to someone else
Perhaps they belong to my grandmother
She could have had hands like these
I watched her smooth the hair of a grandchild
whose head was in her lap

She had hands that patted a chair
next to hers, when she wanted you to sit
Hands that spread mayonnaise
on wheat bread
Scooped ice cream
That needle-pointed seat cushions
They were good for pouring tea

She had hands that picked peas
from long vines that grew
in the fenced garden
Hands that held the hose
that watered yellow roses
she clipped and dropped into a vase
to brighten the room

She had hands like leather
from so much sun
Hands that bridled horses
That carried a saddle and cinched it
Then lifted a small child
up on a horse
for the very first time

She had hands like these

Stone in My Pocket

I carry a small stone in my pocket
to remind me I borrow this land
These trees are here as shelter
for the chickadees I feed
And the downed pines
with their nooks for field mice
The tall-standing dead fir –
a haven for the woodpecker
who beats his drum and
gives me a new rhythm

This small stone in my pocket
is smooth like the sun in June
Hard like pond ice
in February
Warm from riding against my thigh
and smooth like the crust of bread
fresh from the oven

This stone anchors me to what is here
Sun filtering through trees across the yard
Water in the pond lapping against the ice
The snow dropping into my glove
as I slip it on

This stone was given to me
by a child who is able
to love its color
give it a name
and to paint it with the memory
of one summer day

The Bubbles

Enough

Later,
if I become feeble,
need to relinquish my days
to the care of others,
will it be enough to remember:

the cardinal perched high
in the backyard pine
as he preened his scarlet feathers
then sang a proud song,

the Rosas Rugosa
that surrounded our deck,
daily took away my breath
with their heady fragrance,

and so many lush strawberries
plucked fresh from our garden,
sliced and heaped on warm shortcakes,
then topped with freshly whipped cream?

If I am feeble,
need to relinquish my days
to the care of others,
will it all be enough
to remember?

Selkie O'Mira

My Friend

I leave my worries in a basket on your doorstep.
They can wait while we have tea and
                         oh, you've made cookies . . .

If I forget them when I go, never mind.
You could toss them in your compost bin,
set the basket out for a bird's nest
or use it to gather flowers for your
                         lovely table . . .

Janet L. G. G. Smith

An Old Picture

In the hot attic,
of this dog day afternoon,
I rummage through a battered
trunk, find a birthday picture
of my mother, gone twelve years.

As remembered, she's beautiful,
wearing her wide-brimmed hat
adorned with dried wildflowers
from a love-bouquet picked by Dad
many years before.

In this tattered snapshot,
I am holding Mom's hand in mine
as we celebrate her 70th year
of a life lived for others.
I touch my fingertip to her smile.

I see the shocked look on the sweet face
of my three-year-old granddaughter
when she is caught by the camera
with outstretched fingers in
the melting chocolate frosting.

My daughter, Ruth, named for my mother,
holds her infant girl close to her breast
as all five of us lean into each other
in the hot yellow light
of Mom's last day at the lake.

Four generations
of curly gold and silver hair,
wild and wooly in the humidity
of that steamy moment in time,
captured and made permanent
by the snap of a shutter.

Mary Jane Martin

Oh, you brilliant children!

How your laughter
tinkles
as you frolic
in sun splashed waves
wearing
bright colors
that wrap your
berry brown skin.

You
remind me of my
untamed garden
and chase
my cold, brittle thoughts

                                      away.

Mary Jane Martin

Simple Memories

In the early morning
when the world is undisturbed,
stillness covers me like an old quilt.
Even my cat does not break the stillness
as she settles down on me.

In this quiet time,
I rummage through old memories,
peeling the layers as I dig deeper.

It is there, buried in those layers,
where I find forgotten hugs and laughter
from ordinary and simple times:

> Saturdays at Horseshoe Bay
> rare, quiet nights with my mom
> bike rides with my sister
> and marbles with my brother.

Mary Jane Martin

The old pond.
Frogs call to one another.
Croak. *Croak*. Croak.

August Recollection – Age Eight

Early morning sweat
on sticky sheets
clings to my shoulder
as I climb out of bed
Sweet smell of geranium
lifts up
through second floor windows
I scamper down the stairs
where yesterday's mown grass
meets me at the kitchen sink –
moves in over blowing curtains
to mix with plums ripening
in a clear glass bowl
Crisp newspaper lands on sidewalk
Daddy and I race to scoop it up
Our slow steps
lead back
to thick bacon
fresh orange juice
in red rooster glasses
Mother dresses
mahogany brown table
in morning glory blue placemats
Family chatter quickens
as summer
spreads her arms wide

Selkie O'Mira

Memories of Camp

I remember *Ready . . . Set . . . Go*!

How you two raced for the water.
I held my breath as you flew
over jagged roots and slippery rocks
until you lunged full ahead
laughing into the cool lazy pond
and came up still alive.

I remember how you swam
and swam out to the island and back,
diving for the biggest rocks to stand on,
to claim as your own,
then out to the island again,
coming in to compare pruney hands.

You lived in your towels those summers,
hung dripping on the line at the end of a day.
With no TV, no computer at camp,
we listened to music or made our own,
played *Cranium* and *Uno* and *Rat A Tat Cat*
till we fell off one by one into cozy bunks.

I cherish those days as we spend our summers
in town now, where your friends are,
where your social lives demand your presence.
You want to use the cottage for parties,
to hang out with your friends –
we say no, it's sacred space.

Selkie O'Mira

One day you may head out to camp again
to rest and swim, eat and read,
laugh yourself silly at *Uno*,
hike along the trails,
sleep long hours in cozy bunks,
remember how it was.

I remember *Ready . . . Set . . . Go*!

Inside Out

Global Warming

*Everybody talks about the weather,
but nobody does anything about it.*
                    Mark Twain

Is it only me
or is it hotter than ever?
Like a junk yard dog,
I've been a mean bitch
on these hot, humid days.

I snap and snarl
at anyone in my way.
Struggle to inhale
just so I can scream.
Air so thick,
my skin can't breathe.

I've been a mean bitch,
and I just don't see it
changing any time soon.
Even lobsters are shedding
their shells early this year.

Maybe, just maybe,
if everyone else gets
this mean and mad,
we'll do something
about the weather.

But till then,
I'm gonna be a mean bitch.

Debbie Mitchell

Good

His small hand curls around a rock
Arm lifts above his head
Hurls the rock into the lake
Will turns and grins
Eyes afire
Small feet in sandals
Blue shorts askew
T-shirt hanging off one shoulder

He is three
and knows
Throwing rocks is good
Running in the wet grass is good
Finishing your milk is not good
But apple juice is
He measures his day in
hunks of cucumber
a pocket full of pebbles
and blueberries
from a plastic cup

We walk hand in hand
down a dirt road
He stops to watch
as a tree frog crosses
hopping under a log
When I pick him up
He lays his sticky cheek against mine
then wriggles to get free

This boy with busy limbs
will still be with me
this winter when

Debbie Mitchell

he is a thousand miles away
and I find myself
with a few photos
an orange finger painting
and the sound of his voice on the phone
saying
Buzz Lightyear to the rescue

Mary Jane Martin

Gentle rain falls
quietly on flower petals
one drop at a time.

Ash Trees in Autumn

High hopes have I for the ash trees turning in our yard
when Sun beaming through them in the morning
fills our home with a golden glow.
I need this in autumn like I need lilacs in spring.

Year after year, the lilacs fill our senses
with their sweet promise of summer –
their bounty of aroma rules our table.
We drink and drink their fragrance

enough to last a year, and then
some years they're unremarkable –
we've all had too much rain,
the moment passes and is gone.

There are years too, like this one,
when the ash trees don't glow –
they take the short trip from green to brown.
We rake them up and then it's winter.

Oh, but for one – why, I can't say,
one tree in the front yard this year
has gone a different way
is doing its thing, turning gold,

there amidst the browns and grays,
insisting on its own sweet glory –
and Sun shining through its leaves
fills our home with a gentle glow.

Debbie Mitchell

Seasoning

Two years here in Maine
and time is leaving
on large puppy feet
that scamper faster and faster
until they hurtle into
a dive roll down the hill

This was the puzzling
of my parents
They asked where the time had gone
and I answered
with a shrug

Now I ask the question
Answer myself with a deep inhale
A quiet moment looking
to see where I've been

It is as it should be
My smooth-skinned grandchildren
jump on rocks
Sweaty faces, plastered smiles
and I am exhausted watching

My daughter looks up
from her magazine
Half listening to shrill voices
tell of a chipmunk
and a mushroom
and the fish jumping
in the pond

Debbie Mitchell

I perch at the window
cup of tea warming my hands
Watch chickadees return to the feeder
Clouds gathering for an autumn storm

A time of reflection
Each of us
in our season
Taking in air and water
and giving out light

Mirrored Fangs

Camp

In this 7 a.m.
early light
two kayakers paddle
in unison
Late September
on the pond

Swamp maples bend
into red
Days getting cool
I sit in a ray of sun
Reach hands, palm up
to a clear sky

Lift my eyes
to birch leaves
flickering
their own color film
Breathe in pine pitch
and deep, dark mud

This is enough to pull me
into Autumn
and the comfort
of seasons
leaving

Time for locking up
the cabin
Turning off
the water
Time for gathering
red leaves

Janet L. G. G. Smith

Otto

He's not sure if he is eighty seven,
or seventy eight; I'm sixty-seven, I think.
Most days we meet at the mailboxes,
just a short walk down our lane.

He stretches his five-foot-nothing frame,
extends his red suspenders
by using his thick thumbs.

Then he leans into me,
and launches one of his stories
into the snappy fall air between us:

I died right on tha opratin' table,
he says with a look of consternation.
Mah heart just give out and stopped.

BUT, he bellows, *them doctahs wuz smart!*
They took out ma orta, then went out back
to the fridgeratah where they had a extry one!

A orta from a cow it come from,
 a damned cow, by gosh!
Probly one a mine, the farmer says.

So, they took tha ol' one out
sewed in tha new 'un from a cow –
                I think I mighta tol' ya that b'fore? . . .

Then,
Them doctahs, they started ma motah up!
And damned if I didn' come alive!
Yessuh! Right on that-there table.

Otto pauses here for effect. Then repeats
the punch line, whispering:
I did by gosh! Come right alive.

His shoulders, like a small mountain range,
inch upward as he yields this miracle,
this replay of Lazarus rising from the dead.

At this point, he grins, leans in closer to me.
Ya know what I said to them-there
pretty nurses when I woke up, don't cha?

"I don't," I say with a smile, but I really do.
Mooooooooo! Mooooooooo! He bellows.
Git it? he laughs.

I laugh back,
as I do every time
he tells me his story.

Early Fall

Concords

Bunches of grapes, so full and round –
Concords, how they smell like home.
I settle on the porch with a bowl of blue
and eat them one by one –
heady memories of the place I was born.

Where Autumn under a great blue sky
everywhere for miles around
is filled with the sweetest aroma
as trucks full-loaded passing by
are headed for Michigan wineries.

Purple lips and fingertips
suck out the pulp,
spit out the seeds –
a simple ritual that brings me
unreasonable happiness.

Many places I have lived,
an outsider however long I stay –
twenty-some years in Maine now.
And in my hometown I am seldom seen;
familiar faces – I hardly know.

But to go in late September
when Concords drape the land –
rows and rows of their deep set hue –
I know I too have roots,
a place to belong, to call my own.

Purple lips and fingertips
suck out the pulp,
spit out the seeds –
a simple ritual that brings me
unreasonable happiness.

Debbie Mitchell

Sweater-Buttoned Day

Clouds wrap around the sun making
the light lazy and slow to come
Pine needles lay a new brown rug
on the forest floor
Wind moves across the land
from the northwest
Lifts leaves in circles
Brings the scent of oak logs
burning in a reawakened fireplace

Sweater-buttoned October day
Time for moving firewood
For bringing down dead trees
I drag the log splitter out
Lift its arms and slide
the rods down inside
The Pneumatic Lady
inches the wood closer

Right arm, then left
A precision dance
as her nose pierces
one end of the log
and the tension tightens
until the crack releases
last year's sun
One turn of the knob
and she slides open
showing two halves of wood

Circles split
with gratitude
I lift and carry them
Lay them on the pile

Mary Jane Martin

Leaves on Grass

In autumn
leaves on grass
are bright
red
yellow
slick and shiny
like you
slick when you left
in autumn
when
leaves on grass
are dull
brown
yellow
brittle and dry
like my heart
brittle
after you left
in autumn
with leaves on grass.

Janet L. G. G. Smith

The Last Day of October

Criss-crossed breezes
twirl falling leaves,
create a crunchy path
to the lonely cabin
where two hunters
are now headed.

The men, garbed in orange,
armed with rifles and scopes
slung across their backs,
slink along in their red canoe,
slide their paddles in and out
of the gray water's depth.
They head toward the dock
on an ancient shore, now
shadowed by a fall canopy
that soon will be barren.

A trophy buck meanders
from the woods toward
the water's edge, hears
the quiet sound of paddles
slither in water.
He stands tall,
his head held taut.
Unseen,
at rigid attention,
he watches the canoe sneak past,
scans with his wide eyes.
Fear leaves the sinew of his body
sheathed in a forlorn sigh.
He ambles back to the woods,
moseys deep into the cedars,
fully warned before the dawn.

November First

I hunker down at dusk
by the edge of a barren wood,
grasp a glimpse of a tawny doe
meandering across the meadow
toward an abandoned orchard
where fallen apples tempt.

She begins to fade into
snow flurries and shadowy light,
so for minutes I can only imagine
this graceful, relaxed deer
taking delight in the crunch
of a crisp red McIntosh.

I take a step closer
to gain a clearer view,
but the sharp sounds
of cold, brittle twigs
crack under my feet,
shatter the soft silence.

The startled doe shudders
       then snaps to attention, white flag held high,
              signals her flight through November.

Janet L. G. G. Smith

Hot Apple Pie

In my neck of the woods
it is well known
that my 80 year old neighbor
does unto others . . .

When a story of need is told
to him, this man with
a craggy face and sweet heart
fills that need.

Most days, he cuts and piles
wood, a little at a time. Then,
when the call comes, he loads
his truck and delivers.

He lives alone, eats out some.
For the company, he says.
Before Christmas, he slips a fifty
to his favorite waitress, *the one*

*with three young kids and a
no-account husband.* From
his garden, summer and fall,
he hauls boxes of washed veggies

to friends and old neighbors.
At times, when I open my door
to his special knock,
his first words are. . . .

Janet L. G. G. Smith

I don't wanna bothah ya,
but I picked these apples,
thought ya might need 'em.
What I really think is that he

smelled my hot apple pie
from across the way,
not knowing, but hoping,
that I baked it for him,
which I did.

In my neck of the woods,
this small part of Maine,
what goes around,
comes around.

Bob

Was it Bob? It may have been Bob. Someone names the hurricanes so we can tell them apart. I think it was Bob who came screaming up the East Coast that year. In New York, they hadn't had so much fun since The Blackout. We saw them on the news, hanging over the seawall to catch the splash of a crashing sea.

In mid-coast Maine, we took down sails and doubled up lines, lashed the dinghies and secured all hatches. Then we watched. The rain came and the wind. The tide rose and kept on coming. The wind threw seaweed into the trees, rain into our faces. Boats broke loose and danced their way to the rocks. We watched. There's nothing you can do. The wind blew and blew.

On into the night it blew. Then it stopped. It was so quiet. Just the sound of the sea coming ashore. We looked up and saw a clearing in the clouds. And there was the moon, full and bright. We were in the eye of the hurricane. Soon the eye would pass and the wind would change direction and begin to howl once again. But for these few minutes, we stood in the warm stillness and looked at the circle of open sky overhead.

We both saw it. Faintly at first, then growing clearer and more distinct, a rainbow spread itself across the dark sky. "Is that a rainbow?" We questioned the naming of it more than the thing itself for it was as clear as on a summer day, only dark and lit by the moon's reflected light. All the colors were there, from red to violet, in subdued tones.

It didn't stay long; it was just a pause in the storm. But we felt like we were the only ones in the world who saw it. The next morning, we found a few others who, watching over boats or drawn out by the shifting winds, had stood in the eye of Hurricane Bob and seen the night rainbow.

Selkie O'Mira

Accidents

Most accidents occur at intersections –

one should always slow down
 at the crossroads.

Although some problems do arise
 out on the open road –
 moving too fast,
 falling asleep,
 wild animals,

 icy roads can take you down – still,

most accidents occur at intersections.

Bare Room

A room
bare of its belongings
a table
chair
curtains

does not make it empty.

A room
once lived in
is full of ghosts
lingering
with cobwebs
and shadows.

Route 235

I love that –
you come up
over a hill and
there's a car in the
ditch and between you
and the car is a bit of black
ice and in a split second you see
why that car is in the ditch and you
wonder which ditch you are headed for,
hopefully not the same one, then you hit the ice,
your rear-end fishtails, you wish you had thought
earlier of four-wheel drive but it's too late now,
you slide off to the shoulder, get a grip on the
gravel, you're okay this time, you stop,
get out, listen to the other driver go
on for awhile, call for a tow
and the road crew to get
some sand out here,
pretty soon you're
back on the road
on your way
to work.

Blank Page

This page in front of me
is as white and clean
as the snow-covered fields
outside my window.

With words out of reach,
I spend hours gazing
at the frosted field,
lost in its unmarred beauty.

Soon I will take Meggie
for her daily walk
where she will spoil
the pristine field
with her own version
of snow angels;
leave her scent
to mark this field
as her own.

Meggie will be as compelled
to leave her mark
on that field outside,
as I must leave my mark
on this blank page
in front of me.

Janet L. G. G. Smith

The True Story of Santa's Demise
(circa 1950)

Long ago,
once upon a time,
when fall yielded to winter
and its first flakes of snow,
Santa died.

At the age of eleven,
I worked beside my mother,
who stooped over a pine bench
in our brutally cold shed,
wrapping fragrant fir into five-
hundred never-ending circles
worth fifty cents apiece.

Mom's freezing hands,
sticky with pitch, wrapped
the *tips* of double-fir
with wire that drew blood
when tightly pulled.

The only way to make a good wreath,
Mom said in a long patient sigh.
Profit from our work, I learned,
might be seven stockings heaped
with walnuts and oranges.
Wool socks, mittens, caps
and flannel pajamas wrapped
in red tissue, placed under our tree. . . .

Janet L. G. G. Smith

Black winter galoshes
would be lined up
like crows on a wire
for the oldest kids.
Outgrown boots
patched and oiled
for the younger ones.

A carton of camels,
work gloves and a pint
of Seagrams Whiskey
for Dad. *Maybe*,
Mom said.

With my money
I bought four bags of peanuts
for my younger brothers
and Bryl-Cream for my dad.
I gave Mom a box of her favorite
chocolate-covered cherries
and a jar of Pacquins Cream
for her red, raw hands.

Santa Claus,
also known as Jolly Old Soul,
died unexpectedly that year
at his home in my heart,
town of Wells, state of Maine –
age unknown.

Quiet

Janet L. G. G. Smith

Nor'easter

Venison stew simmers
on my ancient black stove
as I ready for this *storm-of-all-storms*.

I've done the drill all my life:
kerosene lamps
candles and flashlights
wooden matches
bathtubs, buckets, and jugs filled.
dry wood from the basement
and coolers with ice ready
when, not *if*, the power fails.
All gathered before
darkness invites itself in,
soon after four.

All night it pounds.
I cry out at its Magnificence,
its Power, my smallness.
I have lived all year for this white isolation.

Tomorrow at dawn,
I will absorb the soundlessness
of swirled snow
settled across the fields.

My brother, Brad,
basks in Florida sun.
Pity him.

Mary Jane Martin

They Say You Can't Go Home Again

They say you can't go home again,
but by God, that doesn't stop
my husband from trying.

Each year,
just as winter and I start to settle in,
he packs Meggie and me into the car
kicking, screaming and barking.

This winter,
he's going back to Duck Key.
Sixty-one miles from the
southernmost point of the US of A –
which is just about as far south as you can get
from my home in Rockland, Maine.

Thirty years ago,
one day blended into another in Duck Key.
Just like the movie, *Groundhog Day*,
each day repeated itself with
muggy mornings, rainy afternoons and
mosquito-filled nights.

So here we are,
back in Duck Key,
still repeating our days.
Each morning,
my husband steps onto the deck
inhaling oppressive, salty trade winds
with a satisfied grin.

Me, I'm inside
where it's air-conditioned,
looking with regret at the
brown spots I spent too
much time working on –
when I was young, blonde
and slender.

In the evening,
with a Jack Daniels in one hand
and mosquito spray in the other,
my husband reminisces
about younger days and older friends.
He would live here again in a New York minute.

Meggie and me?
We console each other with
a big bowl of water
and a tall glass of beer,
as we cross off another day of waiting.

Waiting

Debbie Mitchell

January Lifts Her Smile

This is a hard day
with a cold edge
Bite of the wind
eyes water and nose runs
I walk to the mailbox
Pick steps so as not to fall

A winter of waiting
Snow sits with a crust
Beech trees lose leaves
to the wind
Late January wears
a thick wool hat
Lifts her smile

We wrap winter coats
layer mittens over gloves
move fire wood
Waiting brings
small treats

The hairy woodpecker clings
to suet in cages
Pecks out seeds for lunch
Retreats to a tree

I grill cheese, heat soup
Sit on a wooden stool
Gather in warmth
Then pick a book and read

Small pieces of life
Banded together
A simple time
for living a simple truth

Janet L. G. G. Smith

Why Winds Rage

Raging winds pummel
Mount Battie,
pound the dark harbor.
Renegade waves heave
the winter-wrapped schooners,
garbed in their white slickers.

Raging winds strip
stubborn oak leaves,
swirl them into mounds
soon covered with snow,
like a mother wraps her child
in quilts for a wild, winter night.

Before dawn, their fury spent,
the raging winds quiet,
    then silently tiptoe
        across the white softness
           of a deeply buried fall
                that guarantees Spring.

Janet L. G. G. Smith

Wood, Fire, and Stone
(for Wayne)

He tromps into my kitchen
where bread dough rises,
beans bake, and venison fries.
Then, removes his old mackinaw
with too many burn holes to count.
Then, hanging his wool cap on a peg,
he releases white winter air
of pine-pitch and frigid frost.

Outside,
on the stone wall he built years ago,
he left behind just one warm stone,
where he earlier sat
for his coffee break,
hoping to catch a fleeting gray glimpse
of our January deer
pawing for frozen corn-cobs
in the abandoned winter garden.

Split wood stands neatly stacked into cords,
and the remains from his brush pile,
just a circle of dying orange embers,
indicated his day was done.

Same time
Same sacred place
Swinging his axe
Piling the brush
Lighting a match
Stacking the cords

A man of wisdom owns his days.

Mary Jane Martin

It's about time

we came home
to Maine's winter weather
where my cold Florida heart
warms in relief.

Before we unpack,
he is turning up the heat
and lighting the fire,
already missing
his warm trade winds.

Celebrating *our* return,
Meggie and I head for the harbor
taking our familiar path.

Oblivious to the artic winds
Meggie sniffs and searches for her old friends
while I soak up the empty harbor.
Cold and mist wrap around me,
welcoming me home.

Debbie Mitchell

Midwinter Treat

Once in my life I'd like to eat
a pint of ice cream for lunch
Open the freezer
pull it out and get a spoon

I think the flavor I'd like
is midwinter
With tiny bits of snow
and a hint of pine

It will be layered
with slices of sunlight
a trudge through the woods
and a slide down the hill

I'll eat it very slowly
despite my hunger
I'll memorize each bite
and savor each sound

And when I've finished
I'll lick the carton clean
and start dreaming
of a flavor for June

Memories